HATHOR

EGYPTIAN GODDESS OF MANY NAMES

by Tammy Gagne

Content Consultant
Rita Lucarelli, PhD
Associate Professor of Egyptology
University of California, Berkeley
Berkeley, CA

CAPSTONE PRESS
a capstone imprint

Snap Books are published by Capstone Press,
1710 Roe Crest Drive, North Mankato, Minnesota 56003
www.capstonepub.com

Copyright © 2020 by Capstone Press, a Capstone imprint. All rights reserved. No part of this publication may be reproduced in whole or in part, or stored in a retrieval system, or transmitted in any form or by any means, electronic, mechanical, photocopying, recording, or otherwise, without written permission of the publisher.

Library of Congress Cataloging-in-Publication Data
Names: Gagne, Tammy, author.
Title: Hathor : Egyptian goddess of many names / by Tammy Gagne.
Description: 1st Ed. | North Mankato, MN : Capstone, 2019. | Series: Snap books. Legendary goddesses Identifiers: LCCN 2019004857| ISBN 9781543574135 (hardcover) | ISBN 9781543575538 (pbk.) | ISBN 9781543574173 (ebook pdf)
Subjects: LCSH: Hathor (Egyptian deity)—Juvenile literature. Classification: LCC BL2450.H3 G34 2019 | DDC 299/.312114—dc23
LC record available at https://lccn.loc.gov/2019004857

Editorial Credits
Michelle Parkin, editor
Bobbie Nuytten, designer
Svetlana Zhurkin, media researcher
Katy LaVigne, production specialist

Image Credits
Alamy: Mike P. Shepherd, 11; iStockphoto: oversnap, 15; Newscom: Universal Images Group/De Agostini/S. Vannini, 18; Shutterstock: Brita Seifert, 8, Cortyn, 27, Lenteja, 29, LexyK, 24, mama_mia, 10 (bottom), Marcel Clemens, 7, Masterrr, 16, 17, mountainpix, cover, Pierre Jean Durieu, 21, Sharon Wills, 22 (top), Stig Alenas, 4, tan_tan, 5, 10 (top), Zelenskaya, 22 (bottom); SuperStock: age fotostock/Alain Guilleux, 28, DeAgostini, 26; The Metropolitan Museum of Art: Gift of Florence Blumenthal, 1934, 13, Purchase, Dr. and Mrs. Edmundo Lasalle Gift, 1968, 9 (top), Rogers Fund, 1911, 20

Illustrations by Alessandra Fusi
Design Elements by Shutterstock

All internet sites appearing in back matter were available and accurate when this book was sent to press.

Printed and bound in the USA.
PA70

TABLE OF CONTENTS

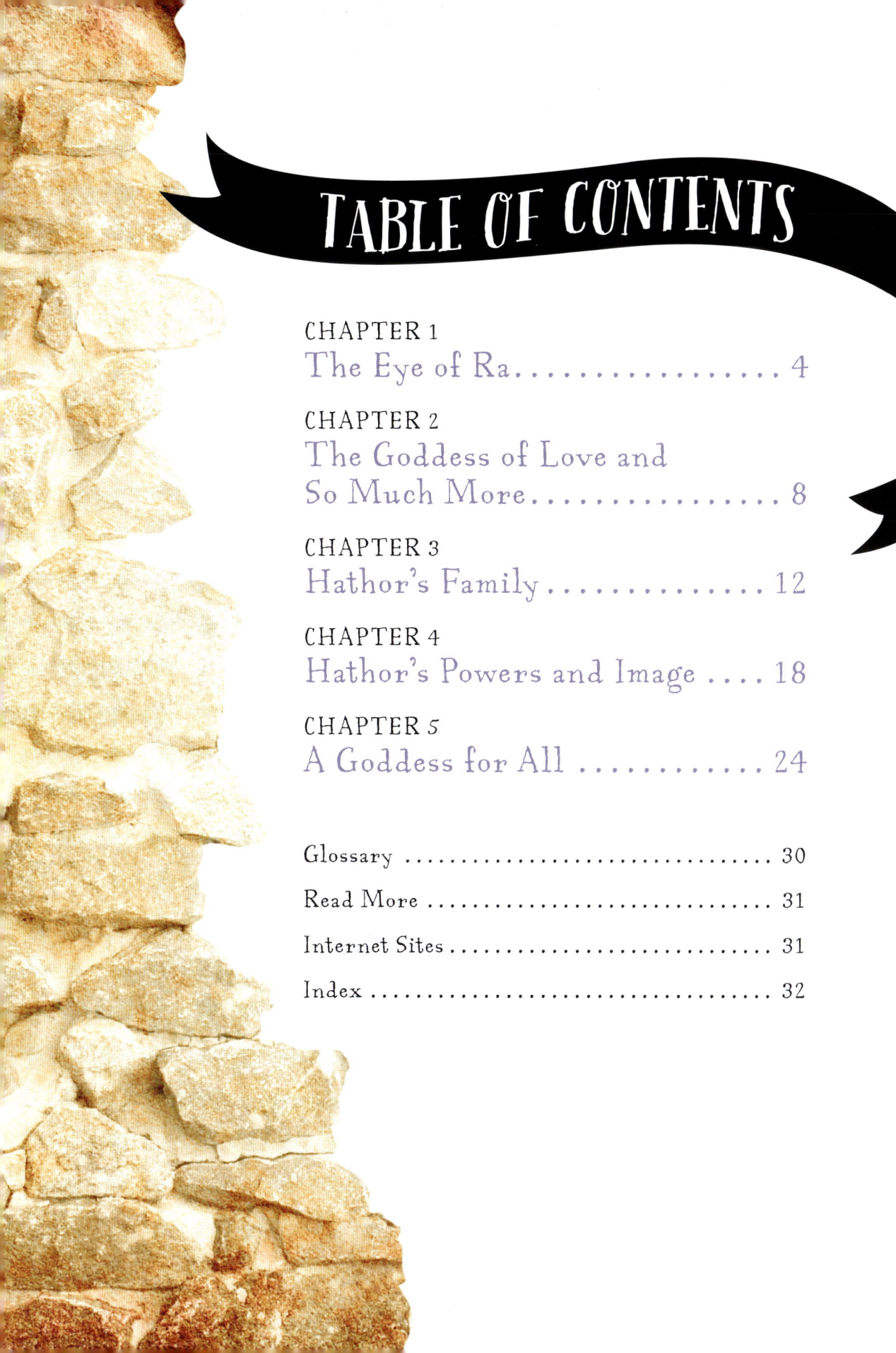

CHAPTER 1
The Eye of Ra................... 4

CHAPTER 2
The Goddess of Love and
So Much More................. 8

CHAPTER 3
Hathor's Family............... 12

CHAPTER 4
Hathor's Powers and Image 18

CHAPTER 5
A Goddess for All 24

Glossary 30
Read More 31
Internet Sites 31
Index 32

Chapter 1

THE EYE OF RA

The world was once an empty, dark place. There were no people or animals. Even the gods hadn't been created yet. The only thing that existed was a great body of water. This was the god Nun.

One day, a shining egg appeared in the darkness. It was Ra, the all-powerful sun god. Ra could create anything and anyone he wanted. All he had to do was name what he wanted to appear. Ra created the earth by calling it Geb. He named the sky Nut. Soon a sun named Khepera rose each morning. Each time Ra named an object, he gave the same name to a god or goddess who would rule over it. The afternoon sun was called Ra. As the sun set in the evening, it was called Atum.

the Egyptian god Ra

Ra was more powerful than any of the other gods. He was even stronger than Nun. But that didn't mean his followers always did as he commanded. Over time, the ancient Egyptians started to lose their faith. They didn't believe in Ra's power and began breaking his laws.

Ra turned to Nun, who told him to create a daughter from Ra's right eye. Ra named his daughter Sekhmet. She became known as the Eye of Ra. The sun god sent her to destroy anyone who disobeyed him.

GODDESS FACT

Ancient Egyptian soldiers prayed to Sekhmet. They believed she could give them strength to win battles.

Sekhmet, the goddess of war

At first, the plan worked. Sekhmet attacked the ancient people as a ferocious lion. Thirsty for blood, she killed everyone who disobeyed her mighty father. But Sekhmet wouldn't stop. She delighted in killing. Ra couldn't control her. If he didn't find a way to stop her soon, she would destroy all of humankind.

Finally, Ra got an idea. He ordered Tenenet, the goddess of beer, to create a strong batch. Then he dyed the beer red. Thinking it was blood, Sekhmet drank the beer until she fell fast asleep. When Sekhmet awoke, she was reborn as Hathor, the Egyptian goddess of love and beauty.

The Lady of the Stars

Our **solar system** is often called the Milky Way. Egyptians believed the Milky Way was made of the milk that flowed from a heavenly cow. Egyptian myths showed a cow with stars around its head. The animal's enormous belly was Earth. Its legs marked north, south, east, and west. Its curved horns held the sun. Hathor represented the Milky Way. She was sometimes called the Lady of the Stars.

solar system—the sun and all the planets, moons, comets, and smaller bodies circling it

the Milky Way over the Egyptian pyramids

Chapter 2

THE GODDESS OF LOVE AND SO MUCH MORE

The goddess Hathor was born, and the ancient people were saved. The fierce lioness, Sekhmet, was gone for good. Her thunderous roar was replaced with Hathor's laughter. Hathor was kinder than Sekhmet. But she was still strong. Only now she fought for love. The new goddess inspired romance. When the ancient Egyptians had troubles in their love lives, they turned to Hathor for help. They prayed for happy marriages. Some even called her the goddess of **destiny**.

GODDESS FACT

Hathor is often compared to Greek goddess Aphrodite.

Music can make people feel joyous. Perhaps this is why Hathor was also the goddess of dancing and songs. Many artists and musicians **worshipped** the goddess. They used their artistic talents as a way of honoring her.

Hathor is often shown with a **sistrum**. This musical instrument was similar to a tambourine, but it was oblong instead of round. It was made out of brass or bronze. Women who wanted to have children played the sistrum while praying to Hathor.

Egyptian sistrum

destiny—the future events in a person's life; destiny is also called fate

worship—to express love and devotion to a god or goddess

sistrum—an oblong musical instrument similar to a tambourine but with a long handle

Hathor was there when a baby was born. She returned when that same person was near death. Ancient Egyptians believed that Hathor helped the dead during the journey to the afterlife. She offered them a drink from the sycamore trees. This is why she was called the Lady of the Southern Sycamore.

Some Egyptian temples showed Hathor reaching out from a sycamore tree to offer the dead food and water.

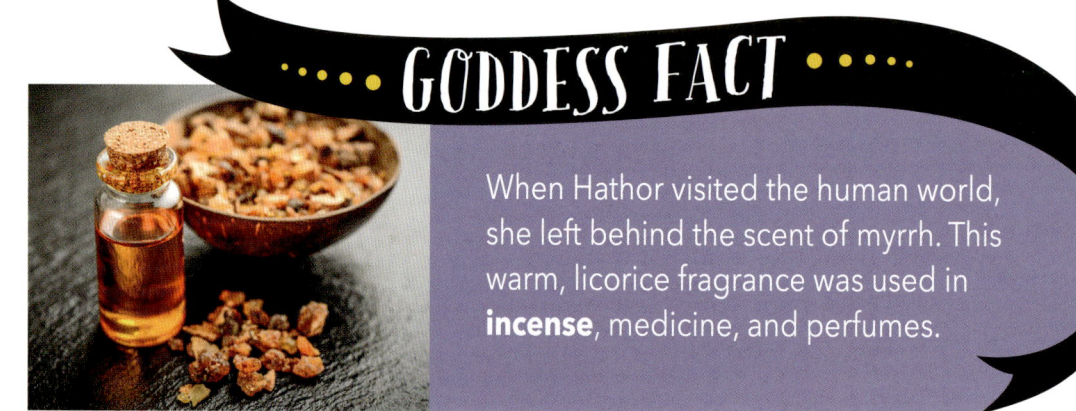

GODDESS FACT

When Hathor visited the human world, she left behind the scent of myrrh. This warm, licorice fragrance was used in **incense**, medicine, and perfumes.

GODDESS FACT

Because of her role helping the dead, Hathor's image was often sculpted onto **sarcophagi**.

incense—a tree gum that produces a sweet odor when burned

sarcophagus—a stone coffin

Chapter 3

HATHOR'S FAMILY

Hathor was created directly from Ra's eye. She had no mother. The goddess's brother was named Shu. As god of dry air, Shu controlled the air between the sky and the earth.

In one myth, Shu's children, Geb and Nut, married and had children. This angered Shu. He pushed Geb and Nut as far apart as he could. The ancient Egyptians believed this was why there is so much distance between the earth and the sky.

The Earth god Geb is shown on the ground. The blue sky goddess Nut is above. The god Shu is the air between them.

Shu's twin sister was Tefnut, the goddess of moisture, dew, and rain. In some stories, Hathor and Tefnut are the same goddess. Hathor's other sister was Bastet. This motherly goddess watched over Egyptian mothers. Like Hathor, Bastet aided in childbirth and guided the dead. Bastet is often depicted with the head of a cat. Many Egyptians worshipped Bastet in this form.

the goddess Bastet

GODDESS FACT

The name *Hathor* means "House of Horus."

Horus was Hathor's husband. The ancient people believed that each **pharaoh** held the spirit of Horus within him. When the pharaoh died, Horus's spirit left his body and entered the next ruler. Hathor and Horus had one child, Hapi. He represented the yearly flooding of the Nile River. The flooding was important to the Egyptian people. The water made the soil rich enough to grow food.

Becoming Hathor

Osiris was the god of the **underworld**. The ancient Egyptians believed that when a good person died, he or she became Osiris in the afterlife. This was considered a great honor.

When the Romans conquered Egypt around 30 BC, this belief changed. If a man who was worthy died, he became Osiris. If an honorable woman died, she became Hathor.

pharaoh—a king in ancient Egypt
underworld—the place where ancient people believed spirits would go

GODDESS FACT

In early myths, Hathor was known as Horus's mother instead of his wife. Later, the goddess Isis was believed to be Horus's mother.

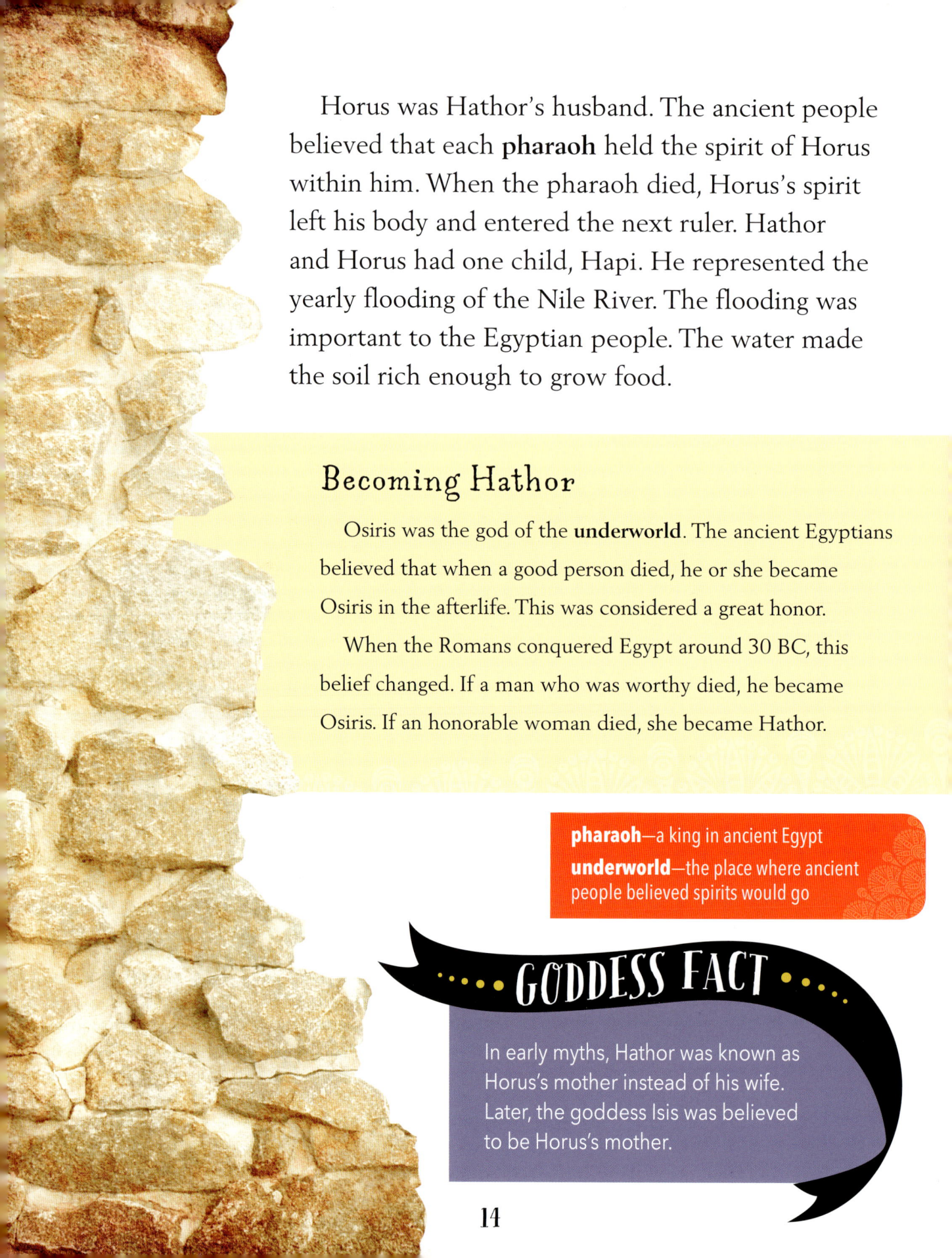

the goddess Hathor

Hathor's Family Tree

Hathor was created from Ra's eye. She did not have a mother. Hathor had several siblings, including Bastet, Tefnut, and Shu. Horus was Hathor's husband. They had one son, Hapi.

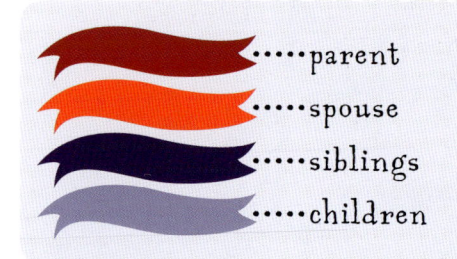

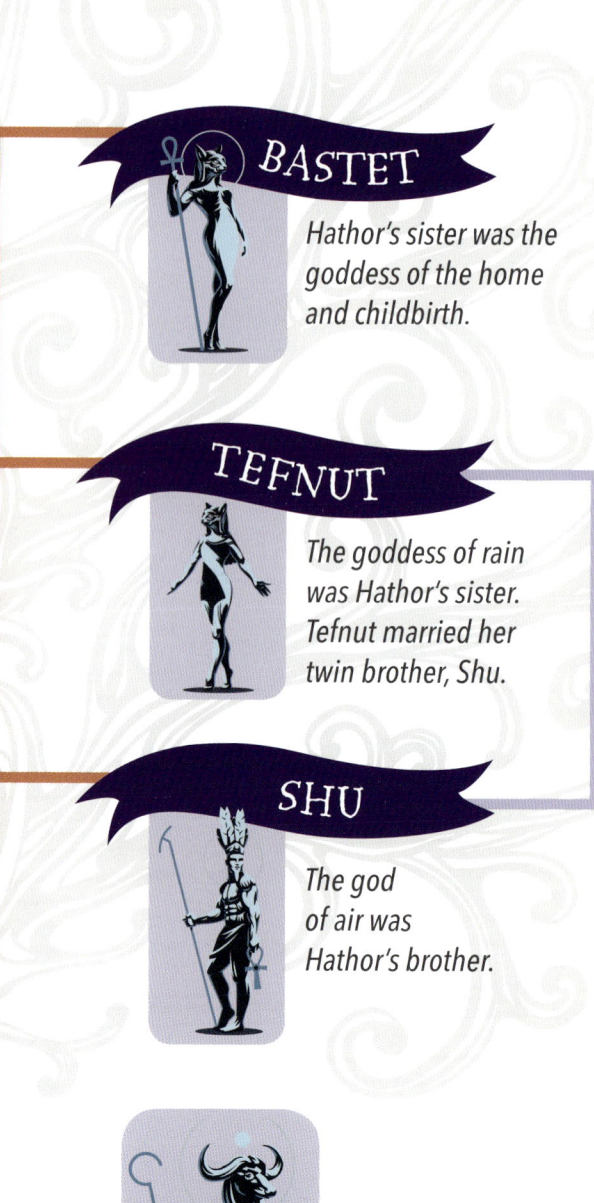

BASTET
Hathor's sister was the goddess of the home and childbirth.

TEFNUT
The goddess of rain was Hathor's sister. Tefnut married her twin brother, Shu.

SHU
The god of air was Hathor's brother.

RA
The Egyptian sun god was Hathor's father.

HATHOR

- ····· parent
- ····· spouse
- ····· siblings
- ····· children

NUT — The sky goddess was Hathor's niece.

GEB — The god of Earth was Hathor's nephew.

ISIS — This powerful goddess was Hathor's great-niece.

OSIRIS — The god of the underworld was Hathor's great-nephew.

HORUS — The Egyptian pharaoh was Hathor's husband.

HAPI — The god of the yearly flooding of the Nile was Hathor's son.

Chapter 4

HATHOR'S POWERS AND IMAGE

Hathor was one of the most powerful goddesses in Egypt. She could do things that no other gods or goddesses could do. When a child was born, she transformed herself into the Seven Hathors and visited the new baby. In this form, the ancient Egyptians believed Hathor knew the child's future, including how long he or she would live.

The Seven Hathors were often shown as seven cows. A painting of the seven cows, along with a bull, was discovered in the tomb of Nefertari, an ancient Egyptian queen.

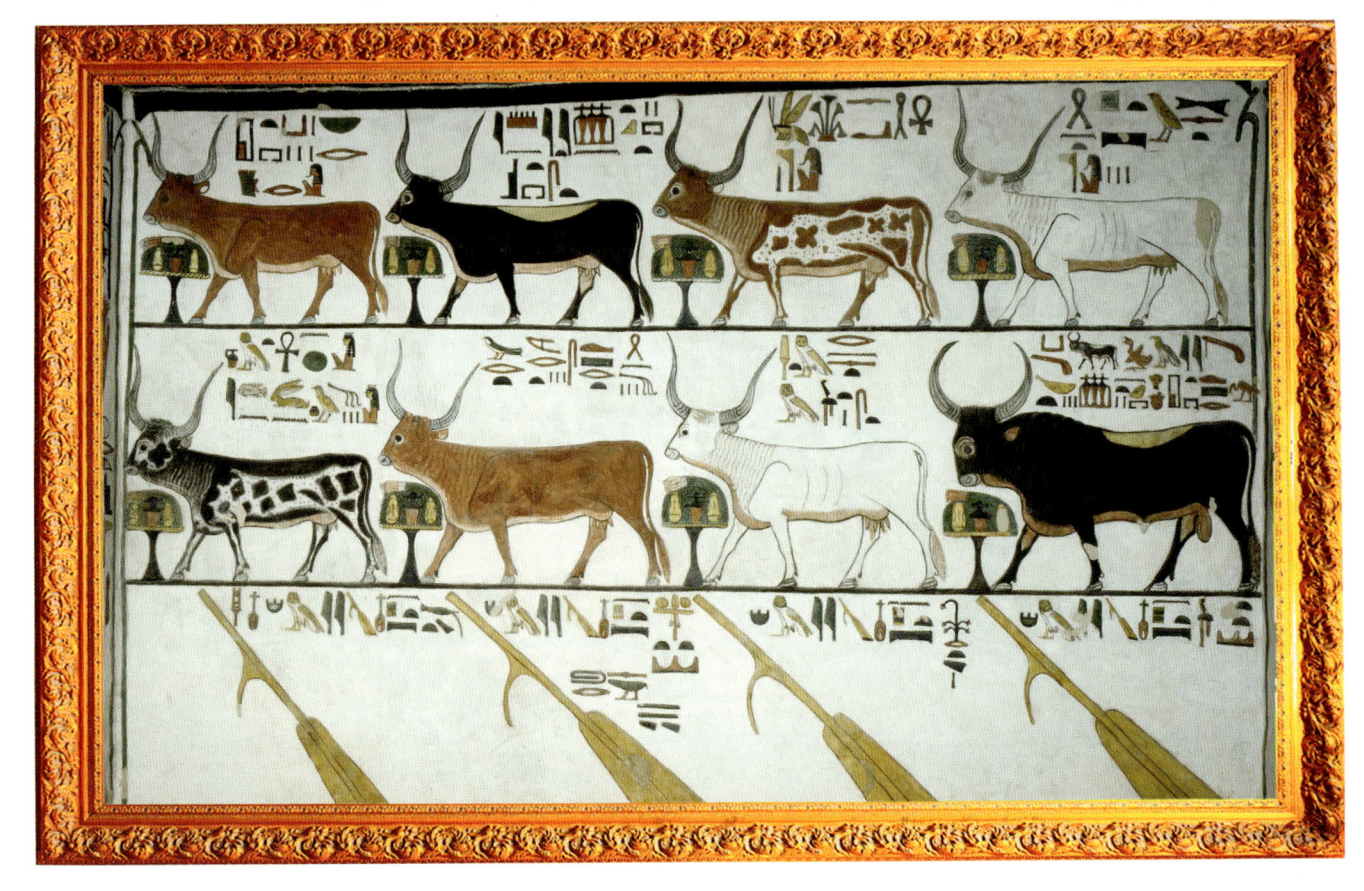

The Seven Hathors could also change the future. It was said that they could turn a bad fortune into a good one. They often did this for Egyptian princes who were headed for danger.

Hathor had great healing powers. In one Egyptian myth, Horus got into a violent fight with his uncle, Seth. Seth was known for causing trouble and chaos. When Hathor found Horus, he was badly injured. Seth had gouged out his eyes. Hathor quickly caught a gazelle and milked it. She then used the milk as medicine, restoring her husband's sight.

THE GODDESS'S JEWELRY

As the goddess of love and beauty, Hathor adored beautiful things. She is often shown wearing jewelry in artwork. Her jewelry was made from malachite, gold, or copper. But she is most often associated with turquoise jewelry. Hathor was called the Lady of Turquoise. This name was likely given to her by Egyptian turquoise miners. They prayed to the goddess for protection in the mines.

Hathor wore a menat necklace. This large necklace was made of multiple strands of beads held together by larger beads. Because it looked like a collar, a menat necklace was sometimes called a menat collar.

Priests and priestesses who worshipped Hathor often wore menats. Dancers and musicians wore them as well. A menat doubles as a musical instrument when worn with a sistrum.

The Great Wild Cow

Hathor is depicted as a woman, a cow, or a woman with cow ears. Because of this, she was often called the Great Wild Cow. In human form, Hathor is often shown wearing a headdress with a red sun disc.

Hathor as a cow with a sun disc headdress

GODDESS FACT

The goddess's **sacred** flower was the blue lotus.

sacred—holy or having to do with religion

Malachite Makeup

Egyptian women wore eye makeup made from malachite. This mineral gave the wearer's eyelids a greenish color. It also helped heal eye infections. Many people believed that Hathor gave malachite this healing property. Mothers put this eye makeup on their babies soon after birth. They believed that it would protect their children from harm.

GODDESS FACT

Hathor is linked to several animals, including cows, cobras, falcons, hippopotamuses, and lions.

Chapter 5

A GODDESS FOR ALL

Many ancient people worshipped Hathor. Her followers ranged from commoners to royalty. Several Egyptian pharaohs prayed to her. The pharaoh Hatshepsut was the first female ruler of Egypt. She built a **shrine** to Hathor in her burial temple at Deir el-Bahri. Male rulers also worshipped Hathor. The pharaoh Ramses II built a temple in Abu Simbel for Hathor and his wife, Nefertari.

temple for Hathor and Nefertari

People who came to Hathor's temples often prayed for safe births. Others sought insight into their futures. Midwives and dream interpreters were found at these temples.

There were both male and female priests in Hathor's temples. This was not common. Most Egyptian **deities** had either priests or priestesses but not both. The most famous Hathor temple was in Dendera. This was the first shrine to the goddess.

> **deity**—a god or goddess
> **shrine**—a structure built to worship a particular deity

THE FIVE GIFTS OF HATHOR

When someone new wanted to worship at Hathor's temple, a **ritual** was performed. It was called the Five Gifts of Hathor. Holding the follower's left hand, the priest would ask what five things the person would miss most if he or she died today. These five things were said to be gifts from Hathor.

Hathor's followers used their left hands for the Five Gifts of Hathor. Farmers used their left hands to grab crops. This hand was always in front of them.

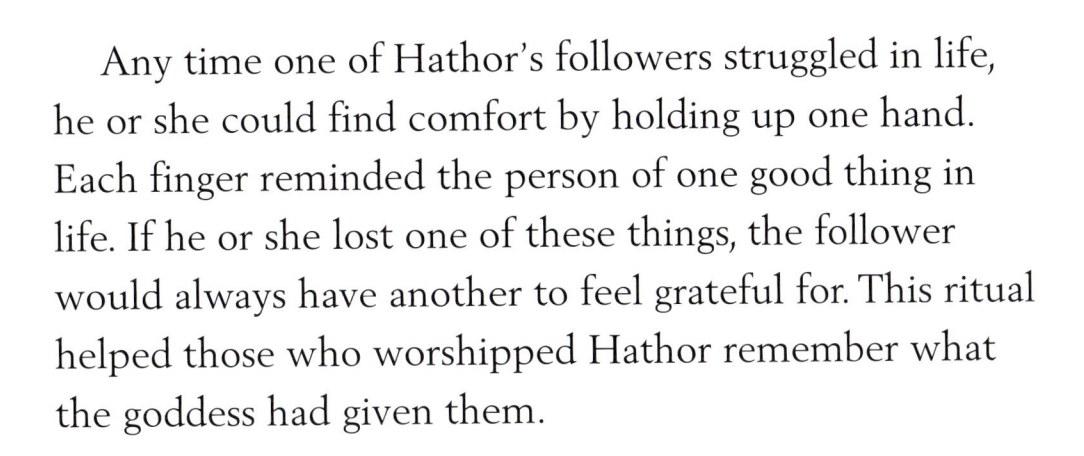

Any time one of Hathor's followers struggled in life, he or she could find comfort by holding up one hand. Each finger reminded the person of one good thing in life. If he or she lost one of these things, the follower would always have another to feel grateful for. This ritual helped those who worshipped Hathor remember what the goddess had given them.

GODDESS FACT

The Temple of Hathor in Dendera is one of the best-preserved temples in Egypt. Inside, it has numerous carvings called **hieroglyphics**.

ritual—an action or prayer carried out by a priest or worshippers

hieroglyphic—a picture or symbol used in the ancient Egyptian system of writing

FESTIVALS

In ancient times, many festivals were held in Hathor's honor. They included the Feast of Hathor and the Tekh Festival. People used these celebrations to thank Hathor for the gifts in their lives. Some used the opportunity to ask for her help. The festivals included music and dancing. Her followers would reenact myths about the goddess.

GODDESS FACT

Many ancient Egyptians named their daughters after Hathor. It's believed that Hathor had more children named after her than any other Egyptian god or goddess.

Hathor with cow ears at the Temple of Hatshepsut near Luxor in Egypt

HATHOR TODAY

The ancient Egyptian religion began to decrease in popularity when the Romans took over the nation. Few people in the world still worship the Egyptian gods and goddesses. But a few still do. Kemetism, or Egyptian Neopaganism, revived the ancient religion. It began in the 1970s. In recent years, it has become popular again.

Those who practice Kemetism look to Hathor and the other Egyptian deities to help celebrate their ancestry.

GLOSSARY

deity (DEE-uh-tee)—a god or goddess

destiny (DESS-tuh-nee)—the future events in a person's life; destiny is also called fate

hieroglyphic (HYE-ruh-glif-ik)—a picture or symbol used in the ancient Egyptian system of writing

incense (IN-sens)—a tree gum that produces a sweet odor when burned

pharaoh (FAIR-oh)—a king in ancient Egypt

ritual (RICH-oo-uhl)—an action or prayer carried out by a priest or worshippers

sacred (SAY-krid)—holy or having to do with religion

sarcophagus (sahr-KAH-fuh-guhs)—a stone coffin

shrine (SHRAHYN)—a structure built to worship a particular deity

sistrum (SIS-truhm)—an oblong musical instrument similar to a tambourine but with a long handle

solar system (SOH-lurh SISS-tuhm)—the sun and all the planets, moons, comets, and smaller bodies circling it

underworld (UHN-dur-world)—the place where ancient people believed spirits would go

worship (WUR-ship)—to express love and devotion to a god or goddess

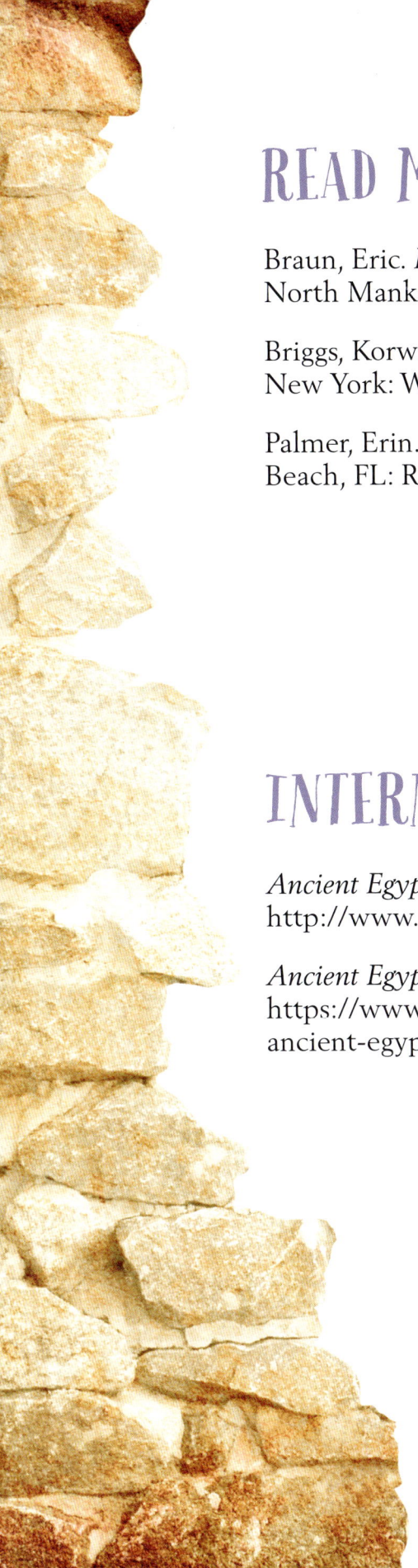

READ MORE

Braun, Eric. *Egyptian Myths.* Mythology Around the World. North Mankato, MN: Capstone Press, 2019.

Briggs, Korwin. *Gods and Heroes: Mythology Around the World.* New York: Workman Publishing Co., 2018.

Palmer, Erin. *Egyptian Mythology.* Mythology Marvels. Vero Beach, FL: Rourke Educational Media, 2017.

INTERNET SITES

Ancient Egyptian Gods
http://www.historyforkids.net/egyptian-gods.html

Ancient Egyptian Gods and Goddesses
https://www.dkfindout.com/us/history/ancient-egypt/ancient-egyptian-gods-and-goddesses/

INDEX

afterlife, 10, 14

Atum, 4

Bastet, 13, 16

cows, 7, 21

Dendera, 25

Feast of Hathor, 28
Five Gifts of Hathor, 26-27

Geb, 4, 12, 17

Hapi, 14, 16, 17
Hatshepsut, 24
Horus, 14, 16, 17, 19

Kemetism, 29
Khepera, 4

malachite, 20, 22
menats, 20, 21
Nefertari, 24
Nile River, 14, 17
Nun, 4, 5
Nut, 4, 12, 17

Ra, 4, 5, 6, 12, 16
Ramses II, 24

Sekhmet, 5, 6, 8
Seven Hathors, 18, 19
Shu, 12, 13, 16
sistrums, 9, 21

Tefnut, 13, 16
Tekh Festival, 28
temples, 24, 25, 26
Tenenet, 6
turquoise, 20